By: Christopher Pindling

This Book Belongs to

_____
_____
_____

First Published in 2024
Text copyright © Christopher Pindling
Illustrations copyright © Christopher Pindling

All Rights Reserved

No part of this publication may be reproduced, or transmitted in any form, or by any means, electrical, mechanical, photocopying, recording or otherwise without the written permission of the publisher.

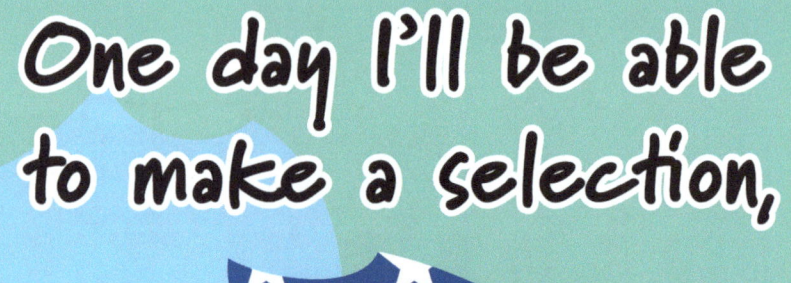

One day I'll be able to make a selection,

to determine who wins the presidential election.

To start off our journey of political endeavors,

With all of the states separated in sections, let's take a look deeper at

LOCAL ELECTIONS

Fighting for what our communities value, We leave to the members of the **CITY COUNCIL**

Representing the county on our political journey, for all legal matters, are the

DISTRICT ATTORNEYS

To manage the finance and all its expenditures, cities and counties appoint

LOCAL TREASURERS

EXECUTIVE

LEGISLATIVE

JUDICIAL

When it comes to the country, to ensure our protection, each state delegates in

CONGRESSIONAL ELECTIONS

435

members combined, based on state population, pass the bills to be signed.

These **100** senators exist in the system, to debate and evolve legislative decisions.

State populations all vary in size, but are equally counted in America's eyes.

Electors are selected with the ultimate promise to vote for their state in the

ELECTORIAL COLLEGE

The executive leader, and our **HEAD OF STATE** is the most influential position to date.

Divided, we're many;
United, we are one.
It's in God we trust
through all we become.

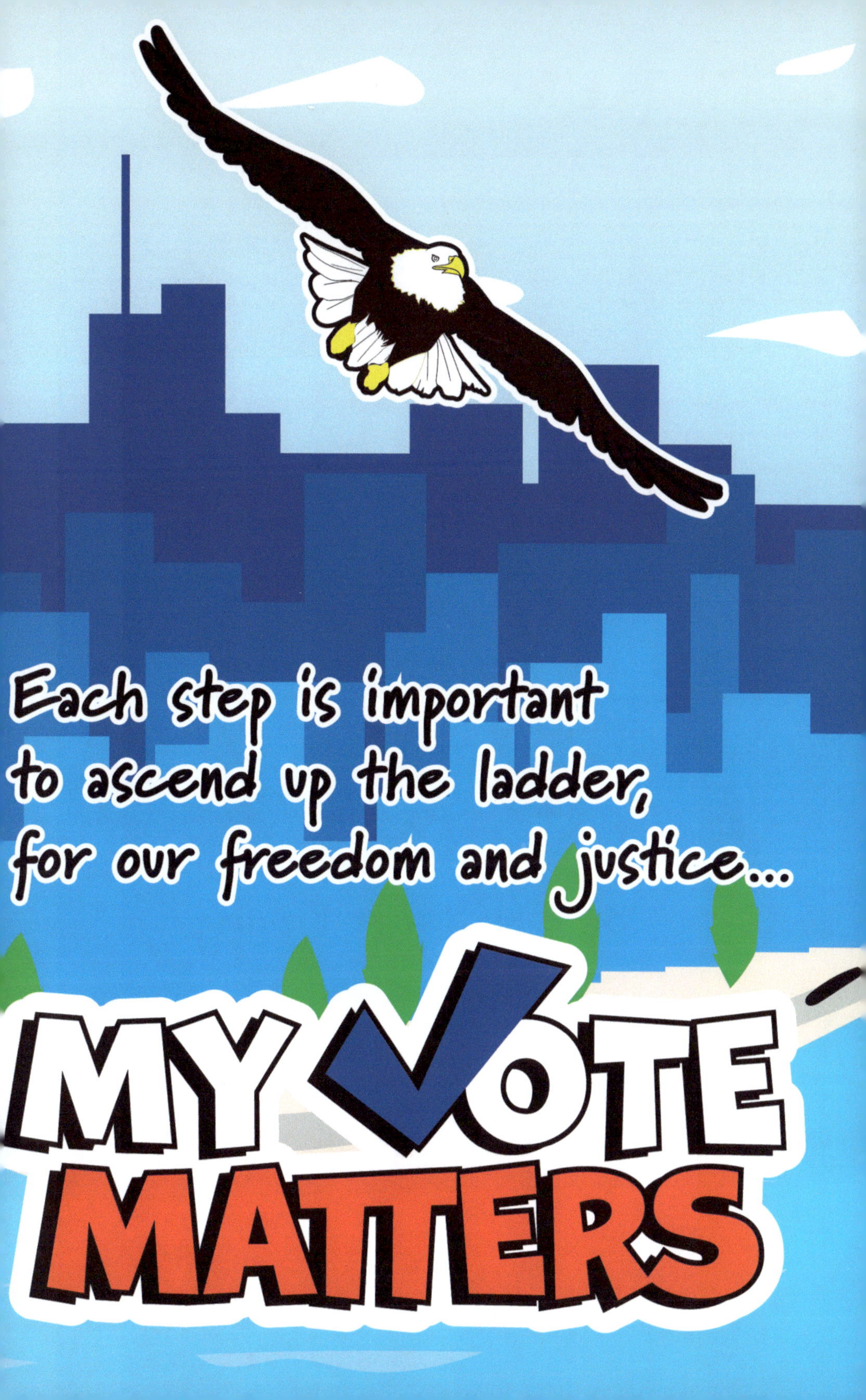
Each step is important
to ascend up the ladder,
for our freedom and justice...
MY VOTE
MATTERS

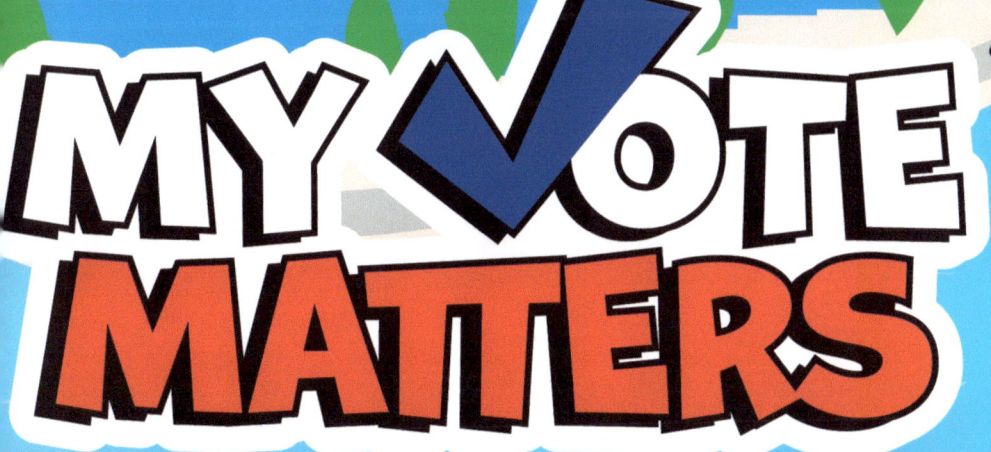

Dedicated to my beautiful son
Dylan Pindling
and all the beautiful children around the world.
BE THE CHANGE!

THE CONSTITUTION

We the People of the United States, in Order to form a more perfect Union, establish Justice, insure domestic Tranquility, provide for the common defence, promote the general Welfare, and secure the Blessings of Liberty to ourselves and our Posterity, do ordain and establish this Constitution for the United States of America.

OF THE UNITED STATES

ARTICLE I
The Legislative Branch

ARTICLE II
The Executive Branch

ARTICLE III
The Judicial Branch

ARTICLE IV
The States

ARTICLE V
Amendments

ARTICLE VI
Supreme Clause

ARTICLE VII
Ratifications

September 17, 1787

BILL OF

I

Freedoms, Petitions, Assembly

II

Right to bear arms

III

Quartering of soldiers

IV

Search and arrest

V

Rights in criminal cases

RIGHTS

VI
Right to a fair trial

VII
Rights in civil cases

VIII
Bail, fines, punishment

IX
Rights retained by the People

X
State's rights

September 25, 1789

AMEND

XI: Lawsuits Against States (1795)

XII: Election of President and Vice President (1804)

XIII: Abortion of Slavery (1865)

XIV: Citizenship and Equal Protection (1868)

XV: Right to Vote Regardless of Race (1870)

XVI: Federal Income Tax (1913)

XVII: Direct Election of Senators (1913)

XVIII: Prohibition of Alcohol (1919)

XIX: Women's Right to Vote (1920)

MENTS

XX: Terms of Office and Presidential Succession (1933)

XXI: Repeal of Prohibition (1933)

XXII: Presidential Term Limits (1951)

XXIII: Electoral Vote for Washington, D.C. (1961)

XXIV: Abortion of Poll Taxes (1964)

XXV: Presidential Succession and Disability (1967)

XXVI: Voting Age Lowered to 18 (1971)

XXVII: Congressional Pay (1992)

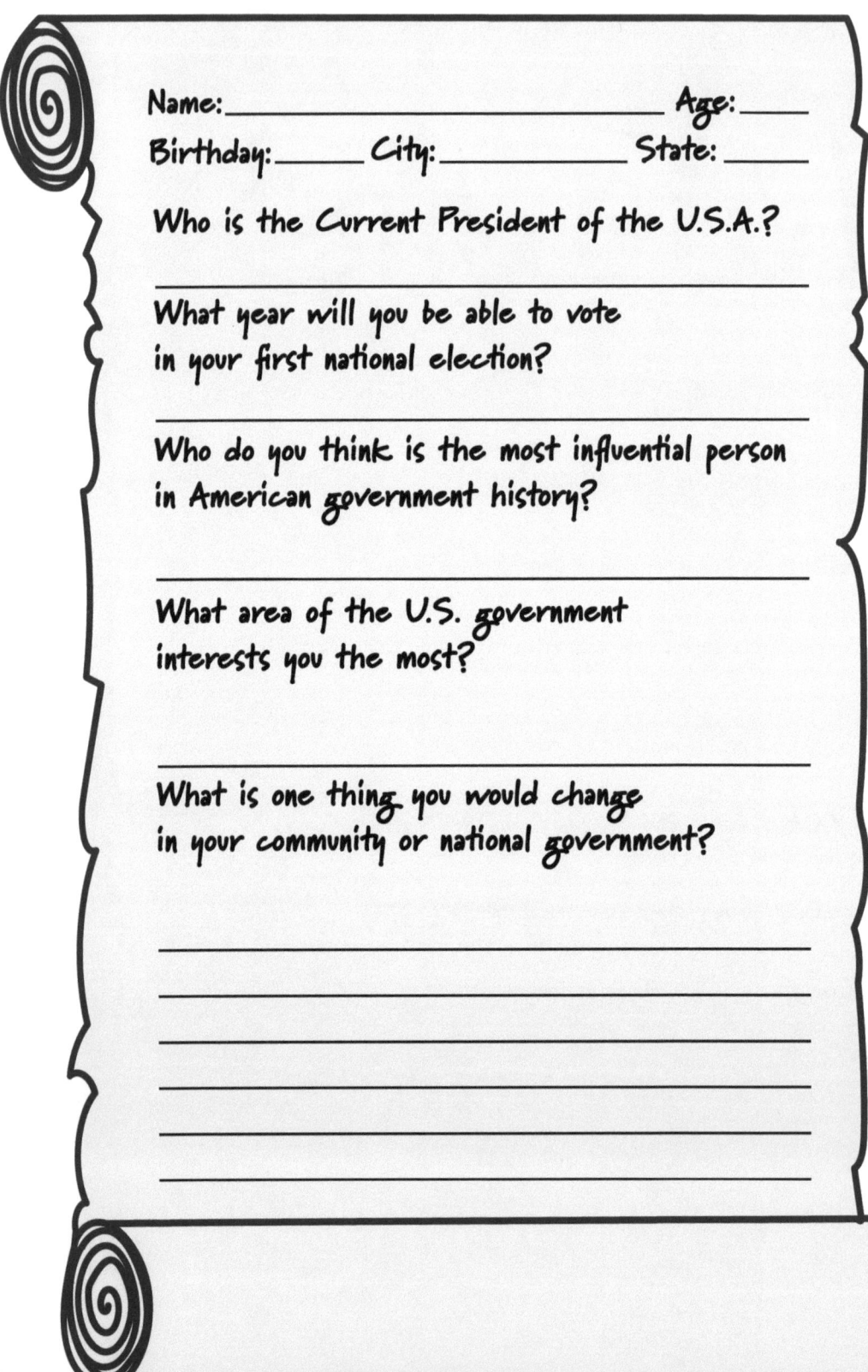

www.ingramcontent.com/pod-product-compliance
Lightning Source LLC
Chambersburg PA
CBHW042311150426

43198CB00006B/113